101 TIPS for Preschool Teachers

Developing Motor Skills

By Barbara F. Backer
Illustrated by Priscilla Burris

Totline
PUBLICATIONS®

Warren Publishing House
A Division of Frank Schaffer Publications
Torrance, California

Dedicated to Patrick, Eric, and Sydney,
who inspired many of the activities in
this book and who bring their
"Grandmommy" great joy.

— B. F. B.

Managing Editor: Kathleen Cubley
Editor: Susan Hodges
Contributing Editors: Gayle Bittinger, Elizabeth McKinnon, Jean Warren
Copyeditor: Kris Fulsaas
Proofreader: Mae Rhodes
Editorial Assistant: Durby Peterson
Graphic Designer: Sarah Ness
Graphic Designer (cover): Brenda Mann Harrison
Layout Artist: Gordon Frazier
Production Managers: Jo Anna Haffner, Melody Olney

ISBN: 1-57029-096-2

Printed in the United States of America
Published by Warren Publishing House

    Editorial Office: P.O. Box 2250
                      Everett, WA 98203
    Sales Office: 23740 Hawthorne Blvd.
                      Torrance, CA 90505

20 19 18 17 16 15 14 13 12 11 10 9 8 7 6 5 4 3 2 1

Contents

Small Muscle Coordination

1 Fingerplays build muscle coordination and strength in little fingers. Fingers learn to move one at a time while you sing and illustrate "Where Is Thumbkin?" It's fun to draw a face on each finger with a washable pen before singing.

2 The index finger, middle finger, and thumb are used for holding and guiding pencils and pens. Children develop practice using these fingers when they squeeze and release spring-type clothespins in this game. Divide a cardboard pizza round into eight or more wedges. Color the wedges with markers. Color wooden clothespins to match each wedge. Have your children pinch clothespins to place them on the rim of the matching-colored section.

3 Using tweezers is also a good finger exercise. Make another game by putting various-sized pompons into a shallow margarine tub. Provide tweezers and another tub. Have your children use tweezers to move the pompons from one container to the other.

4 Provide a container of colored, vinyl-coated paper clips, large and small. Children will automatically hook them together, sometimes practicing classifying or patterning skills while they build coordination.

5 Add index cards to the previous activity. Offer no suggestions on the cards' use. Let your children's creative instincts lead them.

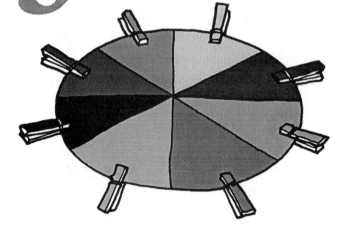

6 Cooking activities provide opportunities to use small muscles. Make a fruit salad using melon balls that your children scoop from ripe melons. Spread butter, peanut butter, or soft cream cheese on crackers.

9 To help your children develop hand-eye coordination and hammering skills, tightly fill a large plastic margarine tub with modeling clay. Provide a wooden hammer and golf tees for children to hammer into the clay.

10 Put spring-type metal clips at the easels. Show your children how to get their own paper, clip it to the easel, then hang the finished painting on a drying line. They'll learn independence while they gain small muscle coordination.

7 Exercise small muscles in the feet and toes. Ask your children to remove their shoes and socks. Then have them roll paper into small balls to pick up with their toes. Try picking up pencils or small toys, too.

8 Put pegs and pegboards in your dramatic play center. Children will use them to create birthday cakes and other delicacies. Encourage your children to weave lengths of yarn or thin strips of fabric around and through the pegs in their creations.

Music and Movement

1 Dancing with streamers elongates the body's motion and provides a gentle stretch to muscles. Make streamer wands by cutting 3-foot-long strips from crepe paper. Fold the strips in half. Flatten one end of a paper towel tube. Insert the folded edge of the streamer into the flattened end of the tube, then staple it closed.

2 Have your children hold streamer wands while they move creatively to gentle, swaying music. Ask them to move the wand high, low, in front of, beside, and behind the body. Have children observe how their movements change when they move to country, rock, or marching rhythms. Move to music from different cultures.

3 Children like glittery, shimmering streamers. Create them by folding a handful of tinsel icicles in half. Wrap tightly at the fold with tape to make handles. Eighteen-inch lengths of tinsel garlands make glittery streamers, too.

4 Obtain large scarves at garage sales. Flatten one against a child's back, then tie the top two corners loosely around the child's neck to form a regal robe. Add a construction paper crown, and have your children march to processional music. Remove the crown and the children become superheroes, soaring to lilting music. Tie bandannas around their necks and watch the children ride imaginary horses to galloping music.

5 Children enjoy moving like animals. Sing the following song and move as the song directs.

Sung to: "Turkey in the Straw"

Oh, you move your arms,
Then your legs move, too.
And you move your body
Like the turkeys do.
Oh, you waddle and you waddle
And you waddle some more.
Then you gobble and you gobble,
As you move around the floor.

Gobble, gobble, gobble;
Gobble, gobble, gobble, gobble.
Gobble, gobble, gobble;
Gobble, gobble, gobble, gobble.
Oh, you waddle and you waddle
And you waddle some more.
Then you gobble and you gobble,
As you move around the floor.

Barbara Backer

6 Use a portable stereo to take music outside. Take advantage of the extra space for marching, hopping, skipping, running, and dancing.

7 Have your children use their bodies to make sounds to accompany music both indoors and out. Clapping hands, tapping toes, and stomping feet are a beginning. What sounds can they make while walking through dried leaves? While sliding their feet through acorns or seashells?

8 Pair up your children for a cooperative movement activity. Have one child move to slow music while the other follows directions to move streamers over, under, beside, behind, around, or in front of his or her partner.

9 Show your children that skipping is a step-then-hop-on-one-foot movement. Step-hop, change feet; step-hop on the other foot, change feet. Do this in slow motion while singing this song, and invite the children to join in. Gradually increase speed. When the children gain skill and confidence, skip to the following song.

Sung to: "Yankee Doodle"

Step and hop and step and hop,
Step and hop and step and hop,
Step and hop and step and hop,
That's the way to skip.

Barbara Backer

10 End movement time with a relaxing activity. After your children pretend they are frisky puppies jumping to catch butterflies and barking at cats, have them yawn, stretch their puppy backs, then plop down on the floor. Slowly, they curl up, pulling back paws under their bodies. Finally, have them place puppy heads on their front paws, and rest.

Dressing Skills

1 Encourage parents to dress children in easy-to-manage clothing. Children are more likely to attempt to dress themselves when their clothing is easy to put on and take off. Avoid belts, pants with stiff snaps, and overalls with hard-to-open snaps and buttons. Best choices are elastic-waist pants and pullover knit shirts.

2 For stubborn zippers and reluctant snaps—usually found on jeans—rub the metal zipper with a pencil point. (The graphite lubricates the metal.) For reluctant snaps, stick the pencil point into the metal snap's top and run it round and round. This must be repeated after each washing.

3 For ease in putting on shoes, tell a child that the shoe is a monster. The opening is its mouth; the shoe's tongue is the monster's tongue. The monster must open its mouth very wide and lift its tongue to get the foot in. Then it puts down its tongue and (as laces are pulled tight) closes its teeth.

4 Children can put on their jackets independently. Lay the jacket on its back on the floor. Spread open the front. Have the child lie down on top of the jacket, slip his or her arms into the jacket's arms, and stand up.

5 Show your children how buttons work—by sliding them sideways through the buttonhole. Help them see that tugging on a garment or using a "ripping" motion won't work. Slightly stretch the buttonholes of clothes in the dramatic play center to make them easier to button.

6 In the dramatic play center, provide dolls of various sizes and an assortment of clothing for each one. Include clothes that have a variety of fasteners, including large and small snaps, large hook-and-eye closings, zippers, and Velcro. On "dress-up" garments, replace tiny snaps or tiny hooks and eyes with larger ones.

7 Begin to teach zipping when children first wear cool-weather jackets that have big zippers. Show your children, one at a time, how to bring the zipper's pull to the bottom, flatten the pull, and hold it closed. Show them the long, thin opening this creates, and the long, thin end of the zipper's other side that will slide into this opening. Demonstrate sliding one side into the other, then show how to pull up on the zipper's pull to zip up the jacket.

8 Show your children that unzipping is the reverse of zipping—it involves sliding the pull to the bottom of the zipper's track. Pulling both sides of the jacket apart sideways will often break a zipper, but it will never unzip it.

9 Positioning fingers to put on mittens is easier when children sing this song.

Sung to: "The Farmer in the Dell"

My fingers stand up straight.
My thumb moves away.
I put on my mittens,
And I go outside to play.

Barbara Backer

10 Opening and closing pocketbooks, backpacks, suitcases, briefcases, coin purses, lunchboxes, and other containers gives children practice with zippers, snaps, buttons, buckles, and more. Include these items in the dramatic play center.

Cutting Skills

1 Cutting requires finger strength and coordination. The movements to the following song develop both.

Sung to: "Jimmy Crack Corn"

Open wide, squeeze them tight.
Open wide, squeeze them tight.
Open wide, squeeze them tight—
Move your fingers right.

Barbara Backer

2 Fingers open and the thumb pulls away as you cut. Help children practice this motion without scissors on their hands while they sing the following song.

Sung to: "Old MacDonald Had a Farm"

Watch my fingers open, shut;
That's the way I cut.

Barbara Backer

Have your children continue "cutting" in time to the song, this time with real scissors (but without paper).

index card works well) and guide it through the child's scissors as he or she cuts through the middle. Finally, demonstrate how to hold the scissors in one hand and the paper in the other. To help your children remember to move the paper through the scissors (instead of vice versa), ask them to imagine that their cutting arms are anchored to the table with sticky glue.

3 Once your children have mastered the cutting motion, help them make their first cuts on paper. As a child opens and closes the scissors, glide a piece of paper between the blades so that he or she in snipping "fringe" along the paper's edge. When the child is accustomed to the feel of scissors on paper, he or she is ready to cut paper in half. Select a sheet of heavy paper (an

4 Have your children practice cutting modeling dough to build strength and skill. Designate several pair of scissors just for use with modeling dough. Start by cutting skinny snakes, then thicker ones. Have your children use a rolling pin to flatten pieces of dough. They can cut these with scissors, too. Providing tongue depressors or plastic knives gives another kind of cutting practice.

5 Give beginners long strips of ½-inch-wide paper to snip. Next, give them similar strips that have thick lines drawn across them. Have your children practice cutting "on the line." Gradually give wider strips of paper, and eventually draw wavy lines as cutting guides. Finally, draw zigzags and show the children how to stop cutting and turn the paper in the scissors before continuing.

6 Young ones enjoy cutting paper into tiny scraps. Encourage this practice by providing special envelopes or small bags to collect the scraps in and carry them home. Or save the scraps for collage projects.

7 Avoid using thin, lightweight paper which is difficult for beginners to cut. Use index cards, or ask printing shops to donate scraps of card tag and other heavy stock for practice.

8 Holidays are great times for scissors practice. Give your children the toy and gift ads from magazines and newspapers. They'll cut happily for long periods of time as they select what they would like to receive and what they would like to give to others.

9 Children practice cutting when they use scissors to create Tiger Stripe snacks. (Sanitize scissors beforehand by soaking them in a solution of one part chlorine bleach to ten parts water.) Have each child toast a slice of whole wheat bread. Let him or her cut across a slice of cheese to make four or more strips and lay these on the bread with a bit of the brown bread showing through. Put the sandwich under the broiler just until the cheese begins to melt. Delicious!

10 Children can cut safely with plastic serrated knives. Wrap a rubber band around the handle for a secure grip. Let your children make individual fruit salads. Give each child small pieces of apple and pear, ¼ banana, and a few raisins on a piece of waxed paper. Have the children cut the fruit into bite-size pieces and put the salad in a paper cup. Let them drizzle on orange juice for a zesty dressing, and snack is served.

Weaving, Braiding, and Sewing Skills

1 For first attempts at weaving, give each child a plastic berry basket and a handful of colored pipe cleaners. Explain that weaving is an in-and-out process, and show your children how to weave the pipe cleaners in and out of the basket holes. When they are finished, help them add pipe cleaner handles. No matter how many holes they skip or what direction they go, the results are colorful and useful. Encourage all efforts.

2 Weaving is easier when the materials are large. Have your children decorate a chainlink fence by weaving long strips of colorful fabric in and out of the fence holes. Weave in natural materials like sticks and tall grasses. Use yarn to tie on feathers, leaves, and blossoms. Make this a long-term project. A few snips with scissors make cleanup fast and easy.

3 Give each child a 4-inch square of burlap to examine. Show your children how to unravel the fabric by pulling the strands one at a time. Give each child a small plastic bag to carry home the resulting threads.

4 Simplify braiding by twisting together the ends of three differently colored pipe cleaners. Fasten this end to a fixed object, such as a nail in a board. Show your children the process of alternating from side to side, always putting the outside color over the middle one. These braids make colorful bracelets and other accessories.

5 Make sewing cards by cutting simple shapes from a 9-by-12-inch piece of posterboard. Make holes along the edge, 1 inch apart, with a hole punch. Tie a 6-foot piece of yarn to one of the holes. Dip the other end of the yarn in glue and let it dry to form a "needle." Show your children how to sew in and out or around and around the edge.

9 Show your children how to sew two items together. With a stapler, tack two sheets of paper together. Have the children punch holes along three edges of the paper. Attach yarn to the first hole and attach a twist tie needle (as in tip 6). Have each child make a pouch by sewing around the three sides. He or she can use the pouch to carry home artwork.

10 Attach yarn pieces to citrus net bags. Thread yarn ends into large plastic needles. Have your children sew in and out of the bags' holes. Then have them pull out their stitches. Seeing the sewing process reversed increases thinking skills.

6 To make a quick and easy "needle" for sewing card projects, tie the end of the yarn around the center of a twist tie. Fold the twist tie in half so the ends meet, then twist the ends tightly together.

7 Buy large plastic needles with big eyes at craft or needlework shops. Thread these with yarn. Cut 12-inch squares of burlap and run a line of glue around the edges to prevent raveling. Buy large, two-hole buttons at craft or fabric stores, or cut large buttons from posterboard. Show your children how to sew on the buttons, then let them practice.

8 Purchase plastic needlework canvas at craft stores. Trace a shape or simple picture onto it with markers. Thread a large plastic needle with yarn for your children to use to stitch in and out of holes along the lines.

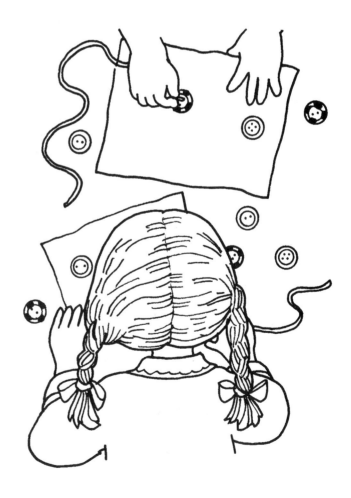

Outdoor Play

1 Outdoor play provides opportunities for children to develop physical fitness and relieve stress. Enjoy a brisk daily walk with your children before or after playtime. Use outdoor space to run, gallop, hop, and jump.

2 Children love to fall down, then get up—again and again. Sing the following song as your children hold hands and move around in a circle. Fall down on the final BOOM!

Sung to: "Here We Go Looby Loo"

Here we go round and round,
Singing a merry tune.
Here we go round and round,
Then we all fall down—BOOM!

Barbara Backer

3 Headbands enhance children's creative motor play outdoors. Children wearing frog headbands will hop across imaginary ponds, while children wearing cat ears stalk imaginary mice. Other ideas include rabbit ears, mouse ears, bear ears, and police officers' or fire fighters' insignias.

4 Have your children set up a variety of pathways leading from one piece of equipment to another. They will enjoy stepping sideways on rope paths, walking backward between lines of empty milk cartons, and hopping between rows of pine cones. Encourage them to make pathways of rocks, leaves, or shells and decide how to move through them.

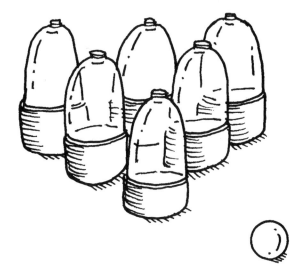

5 Give your children opportunities to rake leaves, straw, sand, and other natural materials. Purchase child-size rakes or cut the handles of standard-size tools to the proper height for children. Children also enjoy sweeping outside walkways and steps with small brooms.

6 Place a Hula Hoop on the ground. Children use it as a target for throwing. Provide beanbags or bottle caps, or challenge your children to use natural materials like pine cones or seed pods.

7 Add music to your outdoor play. Bring a portable stereo outside. With no introduction, play music from superhero movies and watch children "fly" around the yard. Play marches, and see how the movement and play changes. Repeat this regularly, introducing waltzes, polkas, minuets, and music from many lands.

8 Arrange plastic soda bottles in a triangle like bowling pins. Have your children take turns knocking them down with a ball or beanbags. Let the children set up the bottles in any pattern they wish and make up their own rules about where to stand to roll the ball or throw the beanbags. Don't worry about keeping score. The fun comes from actively playing.

9 Children like to draw on pavement with chalk, and they're strengthening both large and small muscles while they bend to draw. Have them draw a path of stepping stones to hop on or a roadway to ride through on tricycles.

10 Sunny days are perfect for building hand-eye coordination while fishing. Put a few inches of water in a wading pool. Cut small fish shapes from plastic bottles. Put a paper clip on each fish's nose. Hang a magnet on a string from the end of a dowel to make a fishing pole. Put the fish in the pool, give your children fishing poles, and let them catch their "limit".

Sifting and Digging Fun

1 Children like to use real equipment. Put trowels, spades, and other gardening tools in the sandbox. Provide child-size spades, hoes, and cultivators, or buy small adult versions and cut the handles down to fit children. Add a small wheelbarrow or cart for moving dirt. Help your children assume the responsibility of cleaning and drying tools at the end of each play period to protect them from rust.

2 To promote digging, paint rocks or seashells with gold spray paint, then bury them in the sand. At the end of outdoor time, encourage children to bury them again for the next group to discover. Let children suggest other treasures to bury, such as milk bottle tops, seed pods, and pine cones.

3 Plastic bottles with handles can be cut into scoops and diggers. Leave bottle caps on. Cut off the bottom end of various-size soda bottles (caps removed) to make funnels.

4 For a summertime treat, have your children put on bathing suits at school, then celebrate "Mud Day." Let them help you add water to a wading pool with dirt in it, then stir and stir to produce mud. Can they tell you what muscles they are using while squeezing, digging, and walking in mud?

5 To reduce the incidence of sand in your children's eyes, show them how thrown sand is carried by the wind. Explain that even though they don't throw sand at others, the wind can carry it into playmates' eyes and mouths. When children understand this, they are less likely to throw sand in the air.

6 Set out a variety of sieves, strainers, berry baskets, colanders, and sifters for your children to use. Have the children compare the merits and disadvantages of each.

7 Challenge your children to make sifters for the sandbox. Provide pie plates, pieces of paper and cardboard, plastic bottles, plastic jar lids, paper punches, hammers and nails (if children are skilled with them), and other items. Encourage all efforts and let the children evaluate the results. Which work best? Which are the most durable?

8 Allow your children to bring cars, trucks, blocks, multiethnic figures, plastic animals, pots, pans, cooking utensils, and other "indoor" items to the sand area. Be certain the children understand it is their responsibility to wash or brush off these items before bringing them back inside.

9 Singing always makes the work go smoother, whether digging or sifting.

Sung to: "Row, Row, Row Your Boat"

Dig, dig, dig the sand,
Dig a hole that's deep.
My shovel helps me move the sand
And push it in a heap.

Sift, sift, sift the sand
In my sieve so fine.
The little sand grains come
     right through;
The big ones stay behind.

Barbara Backer

10 Gritty sand can ruin carpets and floors. To cut down on sand carried inside, hang a whisk broom by the outside door. Children develop motor skills when they remove their shoes, empty them, then brush sand from shoes, socks, and clothes before going inside.

Balancing and Swinging

1 Young children are still developing a sense of balance. Introduce your children to creative movement activities that improve their ability to balance.

Flamingo—Each child stands on one leg, arms outstretched and slowly bends forward from the waist.

Elevator—Each child bends his or her knees and slowly squats down, then comes back up. Children enjoy calling out the floors as they move down and up.

2 Let your children practice balancing on toes, hands, knees and feet with these activities:

Frog—Each child sits on his or her heels and balances on tiptoe. With arms raised, the child lays both forearms on top of his or her head. Can the child hop on tiptoe?

Cat—Each child begins on hands and knees, then straightens legs and arms while slowly dropping his or her head. The child then returns to the starting position.

3 Have the children balance on one, two, three, or more points. Ask your children to get down on their hands and knees. Then ask them to balance with a particular number of body parts touching the ground. Say, "Can you balance with only three parts on the ground? Three different parts? Two? One? Five?" Discuss the various solutions and accept all efforts.

4 Challenge your children to move while balancing a beanbag on a body part. Let them suggest the part—elbow, head, neck, shoulder, outstretched arm, one foot. Can they move from a standing to a sitting position without dropping their beanbag? From standing up to lying down? Can they hop? Walk backward? Sideways?

5 Give each of your children a large spoon and a tennis ball, golf ball, or Ping-Pong ball. Can they balance the ball in the spoon while walking? Walking backward? Try different balls and different sizes of spoons.

6 Have your children begin and end a movement on signal, moving while you tap out a beat on a small drum or a tambourine. When the sound stops, they should stop. When the sound begins, they should move. Practice first while they move a hand or a foot, then an arm or a leg. Now continue while the children walk, skip, hop, or run forward or backward. Can they feel their muscles work as they try to keep their balance?

7 Practice color recognition and listening skills while balancing. Cut 12-by-2-inch strips from colorful fabric remnants. Tie a different-colored strip to each arm and leg of a child. If desired, tie a longer strip as a headband. While your children move to music, call out a color. Ask the children to move only the body part with that color attached. Sometimes, call out two or more colors.

8 Pumping a swing uses many muscles and requires shifting weight and position at just the right time. Sit on a swing that isn't moving and demonstrate how your motion makes the swing move. Help your children practice with the swing at rest.

9 Singing the following song reminds children of the action needed for pumping the swing.

Sung to: "The Paw Paw Patch"

Lie down with my feet out,
Sit up and put them under me.
Lie down with my feet out,
Sit up and put them under me.

Barbara Backer

10 The area under swings quickly becomes worn from children's digging feet. Children build muscles, coordination, and a sense of responsibility when they help you fill in the holes with loose sand. Be certain there is plenty of loose sand or other spongy material under the swings at all times to cushion falls.

Throwing, Catching, Kicking, and Batting Skills

1 All children need safe and nonthreatening equipment while they are developing motor skills. For beginners who are learning to throw and catch, offer soft, slow-moving sponge balls or beach balls.

2 Give your children time to explore balls freely—one ball per child. Next, have them practice throwing and catching with a partner. Show the children how to use both hands to bat the ball up and then hit it forward like a volleyball.

3 Help your children make lightweight balls of several sizes by stuffing paper bags with crumbled newspaper. Tape the bags shut. Use these to toss, kick, and catch. Throw them at targets or into cardboard cartons.

4 A soft ball made from a sock won't intimidate reluctant ball players. Fill the toe and foot of a heavy sock with discarded pantyhose or discarded socks. Tightly tie the leg of the sock as close to the stuffing as possible. Cut off the sock leg close to the knot. These sock balls are good for beginners. Let children gain skill by throwing toward a large target such as a wall or a fence. Space the children so they are unlikely to be hit while retrieving their balls.

8 Learning to kick a ball takes practice. As a first step, have your children remove their shoes and push a beanbag or sock ball along the floor with their feet. Mark a path on the floor with tape, and let them try to follow the path.

9 When your children are learning to kick, start with large, lightweight balls or other light objects like plastic bottles. Let the children kick in any safe direction.

10 Roll several sheets of newspaper into a tight ball, leaving a corner of one sheet hanging out about 6 inches as a "handle." Secure the ball with masking tape. Tie a cord to the handle, and suspend the ball from the ceiling so it hangs at your children's waist level. Flatten, then roll a large paper grocery bag to form a thin bat. Tape securely. Have the children use the bat to hit the suspended ball. Can they hit it while it is moving?

5 When introducing balls, have at least one for every child and extras for when one goes over the fence. When children have to share balls, those with the least ball-handling skill have little chance to use them. If you have a limited number of balls, send only a few children out to play with them (supervised) at a time.

6 A mitt made from the soft side of Velcro makes it easy for children to catch foam balls or beanbags. These mitts are available from parent-teacher stores or educational surplus catalogs.

7 Use plastic lids from whipped topping containers as Frisbees. After your children have practiced throwing and chasing them for several days, place a Hula Hoop or a beach towel on the ground as a target. How close to the target can the children throw their Frisbees?

Using Playground Equipment

1 Accident prevention is the most important part of playground safety. Review accident reports regularly. Records can alert you to danger areas and pinpoint hazardous pieces of equipment or activities.

2 Discuss playground safety and rules with your children. Remind them to look below before jumping off climbing equipment. Show them how the swings move in an arc. While a child swings high, move a large stuffed animal into the swing's path. Seeing the resulting forceful bump helps children understand why they should avoid running in front of or behind the swings.

3 Young children are beginners at coordinating movement. Show them how to use handholds and footholds of climbing equipment for security and safety.

4 It's difficult for little ones to wait for a turn to use a popular piece of equipment. If possible, have more than one swing, tricycle, ball, shovel and pail, and any other especially desirable item. Choose climbing equipment that has many ways to enter so children don't have to wait.

5 Regardless of planning, sometimes children have to wait their turn. To make the wait seem shorter and to focus on getting closer to the turn, sing songs like the following one.

Sung to: "The Farmer in the Dell"

I'm waiting in the line.
I'm waiting in the line.
It's Stuart's turn to climb to the top.
I'm waiting in the line.

Repeat, substituting each child's name as he or she reaches the front of the line.

Barbara Backer

8 Drape old sheets or bedspreads over low areas of the jungle gym to require children to stoop and squat in order to get inside. Divide the jungle gym into areas by draping sheets over bars and holding them in place with clothespins, as in the illustration.

9 Metal slides can become uncomfortably hot on a sunny day. Check these surfaces. If they are too warm, cool them with a sprinkle from a hose. Children enjoy drying the slide with paper towels. Be sure that your children begin drying at the bottom so they won't slip as they climb to dry higher areas.

10 With time, metal slides can become sticky. To ensure smooth sliding, have your children take turns going down the slide while sitting on sheets of waxed paper.

6 Have your children help you check under equipment before they play each day. They can help remove stones, pine cones, and other hazards they may find under climbing equipment and along tricycle paths.

7 Provide equipment and activities for children with special needs. Put sand in large plastic tubs, and set them on milk crates or cinder blocks to raise them so children and adults in wheelchairs have access to them. Large, brightly colored beach balls are easy to see, and because they move slowly, they are easier for slower-moving children to manipulate.

TIP 101

Use Totline® Resources

 When you need ideas for helping young children learn and grow, turn to Totline Publications. Our books are quality, classroom-tested resources for teachers, directors, daycare providers, parents, and others who work with children ages 2 to 6. The innovative ideas presented in our materials challenge and engage young children but need only minimal preparation and common, inexpensive materials. Totline Publications makes learning fun for everyone.